Junior Library of Money

A GUIDE TO TEACHING YOUNG ADULTS ABOUT MONEY

RAE SIMONS

MASON CREST PUBLISHERS INC.
370 Reed Road
Broomall, Pennsylvania 19008
(866)MCP-BOOK (toll free)
www.masoncrest.com

First Printing
9 8 7 6 5 4 3 2 1

Library of Congress Cataloging-in-Publication Data

Simons, Rae, 1957–
A guide to teaching young adults about money / by Rae Simons.
    p. cm.
Includes bibliographical references and index.
ISBN 978-1-4222-1765-8 (hbk.)   ISBN 978-1-4222-1759-7 (series)
ISBN 978-1-4222-1884-6 (pbk.)   ISBN 978-1-4222-1878-5 (pbk. series)
1. Finance, Personal—Juvenile literature. 2. Youth—Finance, Personal—Juvenile literature.
3. Banks and banking—Juvenile literature. 4. Finance—Juvenile literature. I. Title.
HG179.S484 2011
332.02400835—dc22
                        2010031888

Design by Wendy Arakawa.
Produced by Harding House Publishing Service, Inc.
www.hardinghousepages.com
Cover design by Torque Advertising and Design.
Printed by Bang Printing.

CONTENTS

Introduction

Our lives interact with the global financial system on an almost daily basis: we take money out of an ATM machine, we use a credit card to go shopping at the mall, we write a check to pay the rent, we apply for a loan to buy a new car, we set something aside in a savings account, we hear on the evening news whether the stock market went up or down. These interactions are not just frequent, they are consequential. Deciding whether to attend college, buying a house, or saving enough for retirement, are decisions with large financial implications for almost every household. Even small decisions like using a debit or a credit card become large when made repeatedly over time.

And yet, many people do not understand how to make good financial decisions. They do not understand how inflation works or why it matters. They do not understand the long-run costs of using consumer credit. They do not understand how to assess whether attending college makes sense, or whether or how much money they should borrow to do so. They do not understand the many different ways there are to save and invest their money and which investments make the most sense for them.

And because they do not understand, they make mistakes. They run up balances they cannot afford to repay on their credit card. They drop out of high school and end up unemployed or trying to make ends meet on a minimum wage job, or they borrow so much to pay for college that they are drowning in debt when they graduate. They don't save enough. They pay high interests rates and fees when lower cost options are available. They don't buy insurance to protect themselves from financial risks. They find themselves declaring bankruptcy, with their homes in foreclosure.

We can do better. We must do better. In an increasingly sophisticated financial world, everyone needs a basic knowledge of our financial system. The books in this series provide just such a foundation. The series has individual books devoted specifically to the financial decisions most relevant to children: work, school, and spending money. Other books in the series introduce students to the key institutions of our financial system: money, banks, the stock market, the Federal Reserve, the FDIC. Collectively they teach basic financial concepts: inflation, interest rates, compounding, risk vs. reward, credit ratings, stock ownership, capitalism. They explain how basic financial transactions work: how to write a check, how to balance a checking account, what it means to borrow money. And they provide a brief history of our financial system, tracing how we got where we are today.

There are benefits to all of us of having today's children more financially literate. First, if we can help the students of today start making wise financial choices when they are young, they can hopefully avoid the financial mishaps that have been so much in the news of late. Second, as the financial crisis of 2007–2010 has shown, poor individual financial choices can sometimes have implications for the health of the overall financial system, something that affects everyone. Finally, the financial system is an important part of our overall economy. The students of today are the business and political leaders of tomorrow. We need financially literate citizens to choose the leaders who will guide our economy through the inevitable changes that lie ahead.

Brigitte Madrian, Ph.D.
Aetna Professor of Public Policy and
Corporate Management
Harvard Kennedy School

NOTE

This book is designed to be used as a companion to the other books in this series, THE JUNIOR LIBRARY OF MONEY. While the other books in the series are directed at young-adult readers, this book is meant to be used by teachers and parents as they work with young people to help them better understand the various aspects of finances.

1 All About Money: The History, Culture, and Meaning of Modern Finance

Young people need to learn some basic concepts and vocabulary before they can begin to explore the world of money and finance. Most people, both kids and adults, take the mature economic system which exists today for granted. In fact, even that most basic building block of finance—money—is a fairly new concept in human history. Simple early economies, based on the exchange and barter of actual goods, evolved over time and required a standardized currency, coins and later bills, that eventually had little or no intrinsic value itself, but represents a reserve of resources backed up by financial institutions and governments. A basic working knowledge of the principles of how an economy works and the various economic systems—capitalism, communism, and socialism—existing in the world today, rounds out the "ABCs" of finance on which young adults can build.

HERE'S WHAT KIDS NEED TO UNDERSTAND

- Money symbolizes everything that people value. It can be traded for other things that people value an equal amount. In our lives today, this has replaced bartering for different goods and services.

- Paper money was originally I.O.U. notes to other people, and these banknotes became official when people realized paper was a lot easier to carry around than a bunch of coins! Today, a lot of the money we deal with isn't in currency form. Instead, we wire things electronically, using computers.

- Paper bills represent the money a government has. If more bills are printed than money, inflation occurs and the paper money loses most of its value—like what happened in the South during the American Civil War.

- The economy is the distribution of goods and services within a country. This is understood by measuring the GDP (the gross domestic product) or the measure of everything produced in a country.

- There are many systems that countries can use to run their economies, including capitalism, communism, and socialism. The United States is a capitalist country.

ACTIVITIES/PROJECTS

1. Set up a barter system in the classroom (or do this as a class) to help the students understand the concept of assigning values to different items or tasks. Split the class up into small groups and have them barter with each other using the system that you created.

2. As a class, learn about the different economic systems. Hold a class debate about capitalism.

   a. Have half the class argue for capitalism and half the class argue against it.

   b. Have the students do research individually, and then work together to devise a plan for the debate, so that each student in each group has one point to present.

   c. Each student should then turn in a persuasive essay that supports his group's stance.

Suggestions for Parents

1. Discuss with your teenager the concept of assigning value to tasks and time (the way most adults are paid for their jobs). Work together to assign values to household chores based on difficulty and time. Divide chores evenly based on these values—does the system seem fair?

2. Talk with your family about the concepts of wealth, ownership, and the distribution of resources in the country and the world. What seems most fair to everyone? What type of economic system most closely matches your family system?

2 Banking Basics

When asked why he robbed banks, the notorious Willie Sutton replied, "Because that's where the money is!" And to understand some of the basics of both personal and global finance, banks really are "where the money is." The history of banking, from the time of the Ancient Greeks to the highly regulated oversight of today's Federal Reserve, is an evolution toward greater security and safety for people's money. Understanding how banks serve the individual customer, how a checking account works, electronic account management, the value of a savings account— people need this kind of information in order to make intelligent consumer choices. Understanding the language of personal banking, checks, ATMs, interest rates, CDs, and the importance of keeping a balanced checkbook are all vital life skills!

HERE'S WHAT KIDS NEED TO UNDERSTAND

- Banks keep your money safe and offer an alternative to carrying piles of money around with you all the time.

- The first banks were religious temples in Greece that let merchants store their money and cash in notes at other temples, instead of carrying around coins.

- In the United States, the first bank was started by Alexander Hamilton in 1791, but it wasn't until the 1860s that a standardized, national banking system was developed.

- Today, the Federal Reserve (Fed) monitors and regulates all the banks in the country.

- Checks act like bill notes that allow you to transfer money from one bank account to another.

- Electronic banking lets you access your account 24 hours a day—not just when the banks are open during business hours.

- Balancing your checkbook is important to make sure you don't spend money you don't have.

- While checking accounts give you easy access to money you want to spend almost every day, saving accounts let you save money while earning interest.

ACTIVITIES/PROJECTS

1. Make up several mock checks and distribute them to the class. Tell the class that each student has a checking account and a checkbook. Have students write checks for a few different kinds of payments (rent, utilities, etc.), making sure that they understand each aspect of filling out a check.

2. Have the students write down the amount of their checks and the reason for the spending in a mock check ledger. Give each student a starting balance from which to work. Make sure that they write down each check that they write and then have them subtract that amount from their starting balance. At the end of the activity, have students go over their check ledgers and make sure that their total at the end is the same as other students.

Talk About It

Banks help people manage their money effectively, ensuring that it's safe and available when needed. What are the benefits of having a bank account? How would you use a bank account if you had one? When might you use a check? When would you use a debit card? When would you take out cash?

Suggestions for Parents

1. Have your teen keep track of all the spending she does and the money she's earned, in the same way that you might keep a check ledger. Help her understand the importance of keeping track of her purchases when she makes them, so that she doesn't forget to take some spending into account. Let her know that getting into the habit of writing down the reason for the spending she does is also important. At the end of a set amount of time, work with your teen to go over all of the spending and earning that she's written down, working to "balance" her ledger, ensuring that her spending, earning, and total add up correctly.

2. After discussing the benefits of keeping money in a savings account (where money will earn interest), consider having your teenager "deposit" money into the First Bank of Your Family. If you give him an allowance, have him put aside a set amount into his savings account (10 percent is often a good starting point). Work out an interest rate with your teen and make sure he understands interest. When you and your teenager feel he's ready to do so, help him open his own savings account at your local bank.

3 The Cost of Living

Parents, and teachers, too, can sometimes find themselves being frustrated with many young people's lack of understanding of what things cost, and why. In order to begin to learn to be economically knowledgeable and responsible adults, kids need to develop a sense of what grownups have been calling for centuries "the value of money," how basic a necessity it is for living in the modern world. Appreciating the elements that make up the cost of living—food, housing, clothing, transportation, education, medical care, and all of the extras—can help kids learn to value what things cost in the real world and—maybe!—not take these things for granted. Learning how the cost of living is affected by economic conditions and how it can vary at different times and in different places can help young people better understand the economic context in which they live.

HERE'S WHAT KIDS NEED TO UNDERSTAND

- The cost of living is the amount of money a person needs to spend on housing, food, transportation, clothing, and other items they need to live. Cost of living isn't an exact amount of money, and doesn't mean that's all the money a person needs to live the way he wants, but rather it is a term referring to the amount of money a person spends throughout daily life.

- To get a sense of your cost of living you must consider how much you spend on housing, food, clothing, transportation, entertainment, medical care, and a wide variety of other costs. The amount you spend on each of these categories is factored into your cost of living.

- The cost of living isn't a set amount of money that each person needs to live. It can go up and down based on the conditions in the economy, and depending on where you live. Living in a city typically costs more than living in rural areas, for instance.

ACTIVITIES/PROJECTS

1. Tell students to imagine a night out with their friends during which they go to the movies, eat dinner, and then head home. Ask them to write down all the parts of this night that would cost money. Have students research the cost of each activity, making sure to include the cost of transportation, even if they aren't paying for the gas in a parent's or friend's car.

2. Have students research the effect of inflation on the cost of living. How much has the cost of a gallon of milk gone up over the last 10 years? What about over the last 20? Much of this information can be found online.

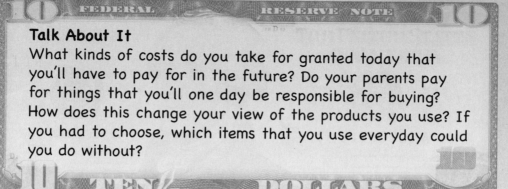

Talk About It
What kinds of costs do you take for granted today that you'll have to pay for in the future? Do your parents pay for things that you'll one day be responsible for buying? How does this change your view of the products you use? If you had to choose, which items that you use everyday could you do without?

Suggestions for Parents

1. Help your teenager create a budget, taking into account all the spending he does. This budget should include entertainment, food, and any other item he pays for, as well as money for savings. Talk to your teen about striking a balance between different kinds of spending and the importance of putting money aside for savings as often as is possible.

2. Go over the costs of living your teenager isn't paying because she lives in your home. Talk to her about the percentage of your income that is spent on housing, utilities, food, entertainment, etc. Seek her input on ways to save money and set priorities for the family budget.

4 Earning Money: Jobs

Getting a job can be one of the most important steps in a young person's growth toward adulthood. With a job, comes responsibility, an opportunity to meet new people and learn new skills, and a chance to earn some spending money and save for future purchases or education. But the working world is a big unknown to most kids, and it's very helpful for them to learn the basics of finding and keeping a job, things many adults take for granted, before they set out to join the workforce. Jobs for young people are sometimes scarce in the modern economy and competition is surprisingly stiff. Helping kids understand how their skills, interests, and education impact their job qualifications, how to look for a job—including how to use valuable personal contacts—the importance of presenting themselves well in a job interview, and how to best meet an employer's expectation, can be a big help in landing that first job. Parents and teachers can offer their own experience in helping young people get off to a good start in their working lives.

HERE'S WHAT KIDS NEED TO UNDERSTAND

- Getting a job can be a great way to earn some money, gain valuable work experience, and get a sense of what you want to do in your future career.

- Though you might worry that you don't have enough work experience to get a job in the first place, consider all of the extracurricular activities in which you participate. Play on a sports team? You're learning about teamwork. Volunteer on the weekends? You're learning dedication and self-motivation. These skills will serve you well when applying for your first job.

- Once you've figured out what kind of work you want to do, try looking in the newspaper or online for job openings. You can also ask the people you know or your school career counselor for help.

- In your first interview, make sure you're giving the right impression. Wear nicer clothes than you might when hanging out with friends. Being polite and professional can help show you in the best light possible.

- Once you've landed the job, make sure that you are aware of the company rules. Feel free to ask questions if need be. Doing your job well and being respectful of others is the best way to impress your employers (as well as your coworkers) and get the most out of your new job.

ACTIVITIES/PROJECTS

1. Bring several days' worth of local newspapers to class. Give each student a newspaper and have her find the want ads. Each student should highlight jobs she thinks she might be interested in. Have each student explain to the class (or a partner if you'd prefer to split the classroom into pairs) why she is interested in the job (or jobs) she has selected. What education or other experiences does she have that would qualify her for that position?

2. Have your class split into groups of three. In each group, one student should act as the interviewer, asking questions to determine what skills the "applicant" has; one should act as the job applicant; and the third student should observe the applicant, giving constructive criticism at the end of a set amount of time. Then students should rotate roles within their groups.

Talk About It

A job can be a way to make money, but it can also be rewarding in and of itself. What do you want to get out of working? Do you want to make the most money possible? Meet friends? Learn how to do something new? What makes finding a job and working important to you?

Suggestions for Parents

1. Work with your teenager to come up with her first resume. Remember to have her list any volunteer work, babysitting, tutoring, or after-school activities in which she participates. Start by brainstorming a list of these kinds of activities. Help your teen organize this information into an appropriate resume format, including her contact information and educational experience. You'll find sample resume formats online.

2. Ask a local business (a retail store, movie theatre, or restaurant) for a job application. Even if your teenager isn't old enough to work, go over the application with him, making sure he understands what information employers want to know about potential employees. Try to come up with some answers to any questions featured on the application. Almost any business will be happy to provide you with an application.

5 Entrepreneurship

The future entrepreneurs of America's future are today's young people. The economic innovation and health of our economy as the twenty-first century progresses will depend on them. Kids are generally very interested in the success stories of entrepreneurs, and adults can help them learn what it takes—that special spirit, hard work, and talent—to start a business from scratch and make it work. Young people themselves are among some of the most creative and successful entrepreneurs in the world today, and kids can be encouraged to start their own businesses, either as a learning experience or as an actual way to make money. Understanding how a business works, how to fund a new business, develop products and a customer base, and how a successful business can grow over time can serve young people well in their personal futures as they learn to recognize and build on potential opportunities in the business world.

HERE'S WHAT KIDS NEED TO UNDERSTAND

- There are many types of entrepreneurs. What they all have in common is that they aren't afraid to take risks when solving problems. The most common type of entrepreneur is someone who starts a business from scratch.

- Kids and teens can start their own businesses. You'll have to balance it with school and friends, but if you have an idea you're passionate about, you can work hard to make your business successful.

- Some of the steps to build a business include coming up with an idea, finding a name, creating a business plan, looking for funding, and marketing your idea.

- If your business is successful, you can think about expanding it beyond your original concept. Who knows, maybe it'll make you a millionaire!

ACTIVITIES/PROJECTS

1. Split the class into groups and have each group brainstorm an idea for a product. Make sure that each group has a name for their product, a description of what it is and what it does, and knows the group of people that would want to buy this product. Each group can also come up with a company name and logo if time permits. Have each student company present their product to the class. At the end of all student presentations, have the classroom vote on the best product and company. Finally, discuss as a class why the highest voted product won. What made it appealing or interesting? Can students see the product being successful?

2. Have students research an entrepreneur they admire, allowing them to choose any businessperson or company founder. A good place to start is to have students research the companies whose products they buy or use. Who founded the company that makes their favorite food, clothing, or media? What was the goal of the company's founder? Do students feel the founder has achieved that goal?

Talk About It

What kind of businesses or brands do you like? What makes you want to buy one version of a product over another? How does a product's marketing influence your decision? How can you apply this to your own ideas for a unique product?

Suggestions for Parents

Talk with your teen about some of her favorite items. Have her use the Internet to find out about who makes and sells that product. Assist her in researching the company that makes her favorite video game, mp3 player, or item of clothing. Take a look at the company's website and examine the marketing that they use to sell the product. Discuss how the marketing makes her feel, or what it makes her think about, making sure that she understands the goal of marketing, company image, and brand recognition.

6 Investing

The principles and techniques of investing may seem a little sophisticated for kids who may still be keeping their money in a piggy bank, but they're not too young to grasp the basics. Teachers and parents can help young people learn the concept of risk and potential reward, the idea of short-term versus long-term strategies in investing, and how different kinds of investments—from the most conservative low-interest savings account to the stock market—can be combined for maximum financial return. Even a small investment now can be a head start toward a young person's future financial security, and tracking that investment over time can be a learning experience—and fun, too. From the savings bank to the "Big Board," understanding the world of investing can prepare young people to make intelligent and informed decisions for their financial future.

HERE'S WHAT KIDS NEED TO UNDERSTAND

- Investing can be a great way to have your money work for you. By putting your money into smart investments, you can add to the amount you have without actually having to work for it.

- Each investment has its own risks and potential rewards. If your investment is riskier, the chance that you'll make money on that investment is lower, but the amount that you could make if successful is higher. The lower the risk, the better your chances of making money, although it will take more time.

- When looking to invest, you have many choices in the kind of investment you want to make. You can put your money into a low-risk, low-return savings account (where your money will gain interest), or take a chance on putting your money into the stock market (although the risk there is certainly higher, the possible pay-off is higher as well). Each kind of investment has its own risk and chance for return.

- Before you invest your money, be sure you have enough to invest. Saving up enough to invest is key. You can save money for investment by cutting your spending, keeping a money diary, considering each purchase you make carefully, and creating savings goals for the short and long term.

ACTIVITIES

Have students write an essay about their view of risk and return. Would they prefer to use their money for riskier, but potentially more lucrative investments? Do they think it's better to invest more safely, but forego huge returns? Make sure each student explains her thinking.

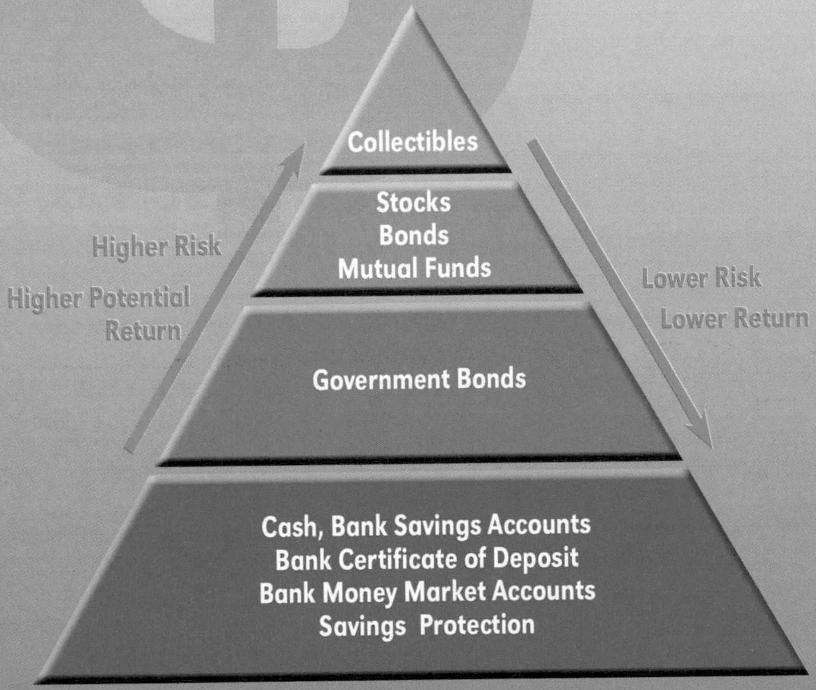

Higher Risk

Higher Potential Return

Lower Risk

Lower Return

Collectibles

Stocks
Bonds
Mutual Funds

Government Bonds

Cash, Bank Savings Accounts
Bank Certificate of Deposit
Bank Money Market Accounts
Savings Protection

Talk About It

What do you think is the right balance between risk and potential reward? Would you put all of your money in a risky investment if it meant you had the chance of doubling it? Would you prefer to keep your money in a safer investment with no chance of losses for a longer period of time?

Suggestions for Parents

1. Help your teen to open a savings account at your local bank. Discuss the interest rate on this account, and work out how long it will take for his money to double using the Power of 72 (divide the interest rate into 72 in order to get the amount of time it will take to double money in a savings account). Encourage your teen to add money to this account as he is able to do so, perhaps 10 percent of his allowance or paycheck.

2. Talk to your teenager about creating long- and short-term savings goals. Does she want a new stereo? Does she want to start saving for a car early? No matter what your teen chooses to save for, help her develop a plan that accounts for her income, spending, and amount she could save. Work with her to determine how long it will take to save for the item she wants. Explain that saving money over time is the first step to investing.

7 Money and Relationships

Most adults know that money and finances can have a profound effect on relationships. Working together for your family's financial security and sharing short- and long-term financial goals can be an important part of a couple's bond. But not having enough money, or handling it irresponsibly, or dealing with debt can be a tremendous source of conflict in a marriage, in a family, and among friends and business associates. Money becomes more and more important to children as they grow into consumers, and adults can teach them valuable lessons about how to keep financial issues in the proper perspective as part of a happy, emotionally fulfilling life. Money is a tool to be used, not an identity. It "can't buy happiness," as the old saying goes, but the lack of money can definitely cause its share of unhappiness and relationship problems. Learning how to discuss financial matters calmly and realistically is a great skill for kids to learn early, and understanding what money can—and cannot—do can be an important step in their understanding themselves and the world around them.

HERE'S WHAT KIDS NEED TO UNDERSTAND

- Money can be a source of conflict in almost any relationship, whether it's within a family, among friends, or between a girl- and boyfriend. Often, different perspectives on how money should be spent cause conflicts in relationships. Each of us is an individual, with our own sense of how we should earn, spend, and save money.

- Whether you have it or you don't, money can stir a wide range of emotions. You might feel a rush of positive feelings when you get paid, but the next day you might feel used when your friends make you pay for lunch. Without enough money, you may feel you can't make as many choices as you could if you had more. It's important not to confuse an emotional issue with a financial one (or vice versa).

- Discussing money with your parents can be difficult. It's easy to fall into other arguments when talking about money, and equally easy to see money as a way in which your parents are trying to control you. More often than not, however, listening to what your parents have to say about money can help you learn about making good financial decisions. Respectfully speaking with your parents about how you feel about certain money-related issues is important as well. Remember to stay calm and express yourself as clearly as possible.

- No matter whether you're speaking with your parents or your friends about money, be sure to try to understand the other person's point of view. Making compromises, rather than having one person give up everything, is key to any relationship, particularly when it comes to money.

- Although money can make you feel happy, sad, powerful, proud, and both in and out of control, you are not your money. Remember that your identity and emotions may be influenced by money, but your money doesn't determine who you are.

ACTIVITIES

1. Ask students to write a short essay responding to the following question: How do you judge a person's level of success? Is money the best way to assess whether someone is "a success" or not?

2. Split your students into small groups. Have each group come up with definitions of the words "want" and "need," in addition to short lists of items that would fall into one category or the other. Afterwards, have each group present their definitions and lists. Vote as a class on the best definitions and compile a class list of items that fall into both "want" and "need."

Talk About It

How does money affect the relationship you have with your parents? What about between you and your friends? Do you talk about money with others, or do you prefer to keep that information private? Can you think of a time that you fought with someone you care about over money? Could you have done something differently to avoid the fight?

Suggestions for Parents

1. For many teenagers, money is a symbol of control, both the control that they have over their own lives, and the degree to which parents still control them. Keeping this in mind when speaking with your teen about money can change the way any conversation goes, perhaps preventing conflict or argument. In many cases, a compromise can make a teen feel as though he's gained some say in his own financial life.

2. When talking with your teenager about money, be sure to listen to what she has to say. In addition, make sure to speak in terms that cannot be taken as accusatory. It may seem simple, but a statement that begins with "I" rather than "you" can take the edge off of what may be simple advice about money.

8 Planning for an Education

The cost of a college education continues to rise (up 5 percent from 2009 to 2010), while in a competitive and increasingly specialized job market, a post-high school degree is more important than ever. Young people need the guidance of parents and teachers in understanding the importance of a college education to their future. Familiarizing them with their options—community colleges, public or private universities, commuting or living on campus—as well as giving them a general idea of how the application process works, can give kids a head start in planning their future education. College costs are a vital piece in this process, and students need to understand the costs of tuition, room and board, transportation, and textbooks, while families should begin as early as possible to prepare for this major expenditure. Understanding financial aid (there was 168 billion dollars available in 2010), scholarships, work-study, and college loans can make the planning process a little less intimidating.

HERE'S WHAT KIDS NEED TO UNDERSTAND

- College is a great opportunity to learn more about the world, become a better person, and make more money in the future. More and more people are going to college after high school because jobs are getting more specialized and need more training.

- Not everyone can afford college tuition, not to mention room and board, transportation, and textbooks. Financial aid helps students and their families pay for college so they don't have to pay hundreds of thousands of dollars out of pocket.

- Getting ready for college takes some work. You'll have to take the SATs or ACTs, pick the schools where you want to apply, and send out the applications. All your work will be worth it once you get those acceptance letters back!

- Financial aid includes merit-based and need-based scholarships, loans, grants, and federal work-study. Fill out the FAFSA form before you get to college so that you're eligible to get financial aid to help you pay for tuition.

- Get creative when saving up for college. Consider living at home, going to a cheaper community college, or get a part-time job to start saving up.

ACTIVITIES

1. Ask students to research community colleges in your local area. How much does it cost to attend these colleges? How much for full-time students? Part-time? What about the difference in cost between students who live in state and those from out-of-state?

2. Have students find a few college applications online (many colleges post applications for prospective students on their websites). Go over these applications and try to create answers for some of the questions they contain. Are there questions that are common to more than one application? Make sure that students understand the language used in the applications.

Suggestions for Parents

1. Speak with your teen about your family's plans for college. Do you plan on paying for her education in full? Do you expect her to get some financial aid? Talking with your teen about how your family plans to pay for her college education can give you time to plan ahead, easing the potential stress of having little time to account for the cost of tuition. Make sure to include options such as living at home and attending community college.

2. If you think your family might need assistance in paying for your teen's college, try sitting alongside your teenager and visiting fafsa.ed.gov for information on Federal Student Aid, money provided to students by the government for the purpose of attending college.

9 The Power to Do Good: Money and Charity

Teaching young people the importance of giving as a part of planning their financial future adds a whole new dimension to the study of money and finance in the classroom and in the home. Researching different charitable organizations, their financial needs and organizational structure, and the work they do can introduce kids to the world of nonprofits and organizations committed to making the world a better place. Encouraging young people to volunteer and donate to charity at an early age can begin a lifetime of generosity. And what better lesson can we teach the next generation than this: that one of the best things about having money is the good you can do with it?

HERE'S WHAT KIDS NEED TO UNDERSTAND

- Everyone can afford to donate something, whether it's money, volunteer time, or used goods. Consider donating old clothes, toys, books, and electronics to those who need them most.

- Helping others, including giving donations to charities, makes people happy. In general, people who focus on relationships and giving tend to be happier than those who focus on money and financial success.

- There are thousands of different charities you can donate to. They work in your own hometown and around the world, tackling tough problems. The first step in giving to charity is to choose one or two organizations that match your interests and work with issues you're passionate about.

- Find a charity that's worthy of your money. Research some charities you're interested in donating to so that you know they'll handle your money well and make a difference in the world.

- Giving to charity makes you feel good about yourself, and helps change the world! Even the smallest donations contribute to solving problems like poverty, hunger, environmental damage, and animal welfare.

ACTIVITIES

1. Have your students research charities in your local area. As a class, vote on a charity that the class can work to help and try to organize a fundraiser to benefit that charity. This might involve soliciting donations after school or having members of the class bring in some money of their own. When you're prepared to donate, make sure that students understand the process, even if it's only mailing a check to the right address. Consider making a field trip to the charity to see how donations are used.

2. Assign your students a short essay about their reasons for wanting to donate to the cause of their choice. Why are they interested in the cause? What drives them to want to give money to charities devoted to that cause? This assignment may involve some research about certain aspects of the causes students choose to write about.

Talk About It

What causes inspire you to help others? Are you interested in helping people have enough food to eat? What about helping to provide money for research on a specific illness? If you had a million dollars to give away, where would you give it?

Suggestions for Parents

1. Work with your teenager to determine what cause most interests him. Research charities that work for that cause and select one your family will support. Allow your teen to be a part of the process of deciding how much you will donate, and encourage him to donate his own resources.

2. Talk with your teen about donating some time to a charity. You may need to help her look into charities that accept volunteer help and what kinds of help she can provide to nonprofits or charity organizations. Make sure that the charity's mission coincides with the causes that interest her. Explain how volunteer work can also be good for her as well as the organizations she's helping. (See chapter 4.)

10 Spending Money

"Money is like manure," so the old saying goes: "it's best when you spread it around." And the real purpose of having money is to spend it. But kids need to learn "how" to spend their money. Making good decisions as a consumer, looking for the best price and value, assessing truth in advertising, and avoiding impulse buying are all aspects of being a mature and wise spender. Adults can encourage young people to be responsible with money by teaching them how to be smart spenders, to think before they buy, and to consider the long-term value of their purchases. Good shopping and spending habits can start early and give kids a head start in mature, disciplined decision-making as a consumer.

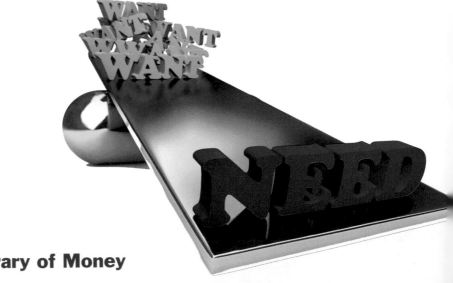

HERE'S WHAT KIDS NEED TO UNDERSTAND

- When you work for a paycheck or do chores around the house to get an allowance from your parents, you're exchanging the value of your time for money. Thinking of money as the time you spent working to earn it can help you understand the value of your time, your money, and the things you buy with it. When you spend money on something, think of the time it took to make that amount.

- Often, all it takes to make a smart spending decision is to stop and think about the item you're buying. Do you really need the item? How often will you use it? Can you wait until it goes on sale? Asking yourself a few key questions before buying something can help you avoid a spending decision you'll regret later.

- Advertising, buying things impulsively, shopping for entertainment, shopping at the last minute for needed purchases, and shopping at the mall can all contribute to unwise spending decisions. Considering each purchase you make carefully is the best way to make better buying decisions without the negative influence of these enemies of wise spending.

- Whether you're using cash, credit, or checks to pay for the items you buy, each form of money has its own benefits and drawbacks. Knowing about each can help you save and spend in the ways that best suit you.

- Spending your money wisely can be difficult at first, but making smart spending choices when you're young will help put you on a path to financial security in the future.

ACTIVITIES

1. Check the price of buying a single drink from a vending machine or cafeteria kiosk at your school. Based on this amount, have students calculate the yearly cost of buying a drink every two weeks, each week, and each day. Have students write about how they would use the money they could save by not buying drinks. Remember to only count school days. Make sure to explain the power of saving even a tiny amount each day.

2. Have students make up lists of pros and cons of using different forms of money. What are the benefits and drawbacks of using cash, credit, or checks? Afterwards, discuss as a class the issues associated with each kind of money.

Talk About It

Of all the spending you do regularly, is there anything you could go without? How can you work to save more and spend less? Do you look for items on sale, or buy what you want when you want it?

Suggestions for Parents

1. Discuss with your teenager the importance of keeping impulses in check when shopping. When you're in a store with your teen, point out the items at the cash register (impulse items) and discuss why cheaper items are placed close to the register. Talk about why impulse buying can lead to unwise spending decisions or cut into money that could otherwise be saved.

2. Work with your teenager to save up for a specific purchase. Help her to determine how long it will take to save for that item based on the amount of money she makes. If she has a job, how many hours would she have to work to afford that new stereo or bicycle? If she earns an allowance, how many weeks of saving would it take to make the purchase? Keep in mind that it's unlikely that your teen (or anyone else, really) could save all of the money that she makes. Make sure to include this thinking in any saving plan.

11 Sustainable Lifestyles in a Changing Economy

It's important to encourage young people to see themselves as citizens of a global community. The world they are growing up in is facing enormous challenges of diminishing natural resources, population growth, and ecological imbalance. In order to be responsible adults in the world of the future, today's adults have to help young people understand how their own individual behavior as consumers and economic decision-makers can have a larger impact. Today's young people are very attuned to ecological and social issues and are a looking for ways to be responsible and conscientious in their response. Teaching them how to have a low impact on the planet, to conserve resources, recycle, spend their money wisely, and be good global citizens can be a valuable contribution to their education in solid, positive values and help them live happier lives in the future. Cutting pennies and protecting our natural resources go hand-in-hand.

HERE'S WHAT KIDS NEED TO UNDERSTAND

- Living sustainably means making sure you and the rest of the world have enough resources to live comfortably in the future. That entails limiting your use of resources today.

- Sustainable living is good for the environment and good for your wallet. By trying to limit your resource use, you also save a lot of money because you buy fewer things and use the things you do buy more wisely.

- One of the most important steps toward sustainability is figuring out what you need and what you want. Once you determine that, you can focus on the things that you need in life. Advertising and impulse buying (as well as the other enemies of wise spending outlined in chapter 10) can lead you to purchase things you don't really need or want.

- There are lots of things you can do to live more sustainably. Small steps include recycling, saving energy, buying secondhand goods, and changing your diet. Bigger steps include limiting your use of nonrenewable energy and living a "slower" and "smaller" life. Bigger isn't always better!

ACTIVITIES

1. Ask students to research how electricity is produced. As a class, discuss the environmental impact of burning coal for electricity. Does knowing about how energy is produced change the way students think about leaving a light on when they leave the room?

2. Have students write a short essay about their thoughts on the differences between being an individual and being part of a global community. Afterwards, hold a class discussion on the merits of global citizenship. How does seeing yourself as a member of a larger, worldwide community affect the purchasing decisions you make? How does it change the way you use the things you own?

Talk About It

How do the things that you buy affect the environment? What about the way you use the things you buy? Do you reuse items as many times as possible before recycling them? Do you limit the amount of time you watch TV to save power? How can you consume less? What small changes could you easily make? What bigger changes might be harder for you?

Suggestions for Parents

1. Discuss with your family about ways in which you can use less energy and live in a more sustainable way. Can you work to turn off the lights when you leave a room? Are the foods you buy and eat made and grown sustainably? Can you make a change in your family's driving habits in order to cut down on gas use, perhaps by rolling several errands into a single trip?

2. As a family, start a "Need vs. Want" journal, in which you classify each and every purchase you make as an item that was needed or wanted. This could be posted on the refrigerator or kept on the kitchen counter, somewhere handy for all family members. Discuss the difference between need and want, as well as the importance of saving money by not spending money on items that the family could go without. If you notice a decrease in family spending, reward yourselves with something the entire family will enjoy doing together.

12 Understanding Credit

As adults, we all know credit can be a blessing as well as a curse. The economic news of recent years has brought this to the fore on a global level. Adults can do a great service to kids by teaching them about the fundamental principles of credit: borrowing, credit cards, bank loans, and dealing with debt. Young people can start building a good credit history early by understanding the pitfalls of unwise, over-extended purchasing and spiraling personal debt. The responsible use of credit can be an excellent tool for consumers, one that kids need to learn before they enter the adult world.

HERE'S WHAT KIDS NEED TO UNDERSTAND

- Credit is essentially borrowed money. When you use a credit card or take out a loan, you are agreeing that you will borrow money now and pay it back later. Credit gives you the opportunity to pay for larger purchases over time, rather than all at once. By taking out a loan on a house or car, for instance, you can pay for these larger items bit by bit each month.

- In addition to helping you make larger purchases, you need to use credit in order to build up a credit history. Lenders use your credit history to decide whether or not you're a good risk for loaning money to. If you have a good credit history, that means you're a responsible borrower, and that lenders can feel certain you'll pay them back in full and on time.

- In order to establish a good credit history, you'll need to make sure to pay your rent and bills on time, and keep your debts low. Paying off your debts is the best way to maintain good credit.

- If you have poor credit, you'll have a harder time borrowing money. Lenders will be able to see whether or not you've used credit responsibly and they will make their lending decisions based on that information. Paying off your debts can help improve your credit.

- Although credit can be a great tool, having poor credit can limit the choices you can make in your life. Making sure to keep your credit debts low and make payments on time can insure that you keep good credit once you have it.

ACTIVITIES

1. Have students look online to find the average interest rates for different credit card users. Specifically, have them find the average interest rate for students, for those with poor credit, and the overall market rate. Using these three percentages, have students figure out how much interest would be added to a debt of $1,000 in one year. Discuss the difference between the average interest rate and the average for those with poor credit, as well as the importance of paying bills as they come in rather than letting debt pile up.

2. Ask students to figure out how long it would take to pay off debts of $1,000, $5,000, and $8,000 by making only minimum monthly payments (set at 2.5% of unpaid debts for the purposes of this exercise). Discuss the issues of making only the minimum monthly payments on credit card debt. Afterwards, ask students to calculate how much less time it would take to pay the same three debts when they paid $25 in addition to each minimum monthly payment.

Talk About It
Do you think it's better to wait to buy something until you can pay for it with cash, or use your credit card and plan to pay it off at the end of the month? What are the benefits and drawbacks of each decision?

Suggestions for Parents

1. Have your teenager choose a relatively inexpensive item she wants to buy and purchase it for her. Work with her to develop a payment plan in order for her to pay you back over time. If she fails to pay, add interest at a rate you determine with her assistance. Make sure to explain notions of borrowing, repaying, and debt beforehand.

2. Talk with your teen about your own experiences with credit cards, loans, debt, and repayment. When you were younger, how did you use credit? Were you an effective, responsible borrower, making sure to pay back your lenders in full and on time, or did you let debt pile up? What advice can you give your teen based on your own experiences?

13 Understanding the Stock Market

Understanding the stock market can help young people gain a broad knowledge of how the global economy works, the structure of corporations, and the role of the individual investor in business. The basic principles of the market and its vocabulary are not difficult for kids to grasp and can lay the groundwork for a better understanding of the risks and rewards of investing in a volatile market. Selecting stocks and tracking them can be fun and interesting for kids: an educated strategy, a bit of gambling, and a certain amount of luck. Today's young people are the corporate executives, brokers, and investors who will influence, and be impacted by, the markets of the future.

HERE'S WHAT KIDS NEED TO UNDERSTAND

- The stock market refers to how pieces of various companies are bought and sold.

- Investing money means to make money from your money. It's a lot less sure than saving money—while you might earn a lot more money than you started with, you might also lose a lot of money.

- A share is a piece of the company that you can buy; each person who owns one of these shares receives dividends each year, or a portion of that company's profits.

- A corporation is any business that splits itself into different shares. In many ways, it has the same legal rights as a person; it pays taxes, can sue or be sued, can own property, or make contracts. It is run by a board of directors who make the decisions for the company.

- The Dow Jones Industrial Average is a measure of how thirty large stocks are doing. It serves as a measure for the strength of the rest of the stock market as well.

- A "bull-market" means a time when the stock market is doing well and the values of stocks are increasing, while a "bear-market" is the opposite.

- The stock market and the economy are connected; when one is doing well, so is the other.

ACTIVITIES

1. Give each of your students a set amount of imaginary money. Ask students to put half their imaginary money into a "savings account" where it will get 4 percent interest, while they "invest" the other half in one or more stocks, selecting companies in which they have confidence. Students should research the price of a share and determine how many shares of which companies they can afford with their money, giving them the option to save some of the money they've been given. Over time, have students track their stocks as they go up or down (either online or in newspapers). After a set amount of time (a few weeks, perhaps), have students assess their losses or earnings. How did their stocks do? Which earned more money, their savings accounts or their investments in the stock market? Was it better to invest in a single stock or invest in a variety of stocks?

2. Have students select a single company to watch on the stock exchange. This might include reports each day or each week about the rise or fall of the stock of their selected company. Was there a specific reason for the stock price rising or falling?

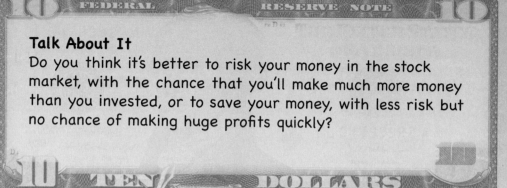

Talk About It
Do you think it's better to risk your money in the stock market, with the chance that you'll make much more money than you invested, or to save your money, with less risk but no chance of making huge profits quickly?

Suggestions for Parents

1. If you've invested in the stock market, talk with your teen about the stocks you own. How did you decide which stocks to buy? How have those stocks done over time? Where do you get financial advice in order to make investment decisions?

2. Work with your teen to buy a single share in a company. Make sure that the company in which you're investing is one with which you're familiar (or have done research on). Have your teen track the stock over time, and decide together when it's time to sell (in order to cash out or buy another stock). Have you made or lost money over this time? How does this change the way you think of the stock market and investing in general?

OTHER RESOURCES FOR CLASSROOM AND FAMILIES

Books

Bodnar, Janet. *Raising Money Smart Kids: What They Need to Know About Money and How to Tell Them*. Chicago, Ill.: Dearborn Trade Publishing, 2005.

Lermitte, Paul. *Making Allowances: A Dollars and Sense Guide to Teaching Kids About Money*. New York: McGraw-Hill, 2002.

Marquez, Elizabeth and Paul Westbrook. *Teaching Money Applications to Make Mathematics Meaningful, Grades 7–12*. Thousand Oaks, Calif.: Corwin Press, 2007.

Stawski II, Willard. *Kids, Parents & Money: Teaching Personal Finance from Piggy Bank to Prom*. New York: John Wiley & Sons, 2000.

Websites

"Five Money-Saving Shopping Tips"
www.investopedia.com/articles/pf/07/five-saving-tips.asp

"Fun Facts About Money"
Federal Reserve Bank of San Francico
www.frbsf.org/federalreserve/money/funfacts.html

MyMoney
www.mymoney.gov

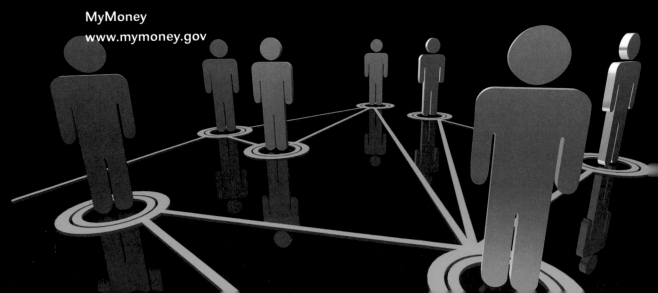

INDEX

About the Author and the Consultant

Rae Simons is a well-established educational author, who has written on a variety of topics for young adults for the past twenty years. She has also worked with financial advisors to produce adult-level books on money management.

Brigitte Madrian is Professor of Public Policy and Corporate Management in the Aetna Chair at Harvard University's Kennedy School of Government. She has also been on the faculty at the Wharton School and the University of Chicago. She is also a Research Associate at the National Bureau of Economic Research and coeditor of the *Journal of Human Resources*. She is the first-place recipient of the National Academy of Social Insurance Dissertation Prize and the TIAA-CREF Paul A. Samuelson Award for Scholarly Research on Lifelong Financial Security.